WINES
AND
CORDIALS

Traditional Homemade Drinks

Compiled by Carol Wilson

with illustrations by
H. Sylvester Stannard RA
and Theresa S. Stannard

SALMON

Index

Cover pictures: *front:* A Country Brook by Theresa S. Stannard
Back: Water Meadows by H. Sylvester Stannard.
Title page: The Old Barn by Theresa S. Stannard

Apple Wine

One of the finest English country wines. Use many different varieties for best flavour.

5-6 lb mixed apples, mixed varieties	**1 teaspoon citric acid**
1½ lb raisins, hot washed and minced	**(omit if using mostly crab apples)**
2 lb granulated sugar	**1 teaspoon Bentonite powder**
1 lb caster sugar	**Wine yeast**
2 teaspoons pectin enzyme	**1 teaspoon potassium sorbate**
1 teaspoon nutrient salt (Tronozymol)	**Campden tablet**

Wash apples in a Campden solution. Empty yeast into ⅔ cup of tepid water, cover and leave for 20 minutes in warm. Remove blemishes from apples, roughly crush them, mix in raisins and put into fermentation bin. Put granulated sugar into pan with 1¾ pints water and heat until dissolved. Bring to boil, cool slightly and add sugar syrup to apples in bin. Stir in 4 pints cold water and rest of ingredients including yeast. Cover loosely and leave in warm to ferment, stirring daily. After 5 days strain liquid into demi-john. Top up to shoulder with cold boiled water and fit airlock and bung. Leave for 10 days, siphon into clean demi-john, add half caster sugar and fit airlock. Leave to ferment, tasting occasionally; if seems too dry add another 4 oz sugar. When fermentation ceased, siphon into clean demi-john, add potassium sorbate and crushed Campden tablet. Keep in the demi-john for 2-3 months, siphon into bottles and seal tightly.

Lavender Cordial

*A pleasantly refreshing, lightly scented drink that is perfect on a hot summer day,
diluted with chilled sparkling mineral water. Avoid flowers that have been treated
with insecticides and pesticides or polluted with traffic fumes. Shake
the flowers gently to dislodge any insects.*

50 lavender flowers
½ pint water
4 oz sugar

Put the water and sugar into a pan and heat gently until the sugar has dissolved completely. Add the lavender flowers and bring to the boil. Remove from the heat, cover the pan and leave to infuse for 30 minutes. Strain the liquid into another pan and bring back to the boil, stirring all the time until the mixture is reduced and syrupy. When reduced, take off the heat and cool completely. Pour into sterilised bottles, seal tightly and leave to get quite cold Store in the refrigerator until required.

Nettle Beer

Before hops were introduced into England, plants and herbs were used to make beer.
Nettles were especially popular. Use only the young tops of the plants and gather
them before they flower as, after flowering, nettles become mildly poisonous.

2 lb young nettle tips	**1 lb malt extract**
(leaves and stalks)	**1 sachet ale yeast**
1 gallon water	**4 teaspoons caster sugar**

Wash the nettles and shake them dry. Heat 2 pints of the water until warm and dissolve the malt extract in it. Meanwhile, put the nettles into a large pan with the remaining water and bring to the boil. Boil for 15 minutes, then strain the nettle water into the malt solution in a bucket. Cover and leave to cool. Discard the nettles. Add the yeast to the cooled liquid and loosely cover the bucket. Next day, skim off the froth and stir the beer. Repeat the skimming and stirring process the following day, then cover and leave to ferment for 6 to 7 days until the surface of the beer is clear. Siphon into fermentation jars and fit air locks. Discard the sediment. Leave the beer for a few days until it looks fairly clear, then siphon into sterilised 1 pint beer bottles leaving an air space at the top. Add ½ teaspoon caster sugar to each bottle. Seal with pop-off plastic caps and leave in a warm room for a few days to ferment the sugar. Store in a cool place for 3-4 weeks before drinking.

Sloe Gin

Probably the most widely known, traditional English country liqueur. The sloes are best picked after they have been frosted so as to get the juice running. However, if this is not possible, put them in a bag in the freezer overnight for the same effect.

Sloes   **Granulated sugar**   **Gin**

Prick each sloe with a darning needle. Half fill sterilised bottles with the fruit. Add approximately 3 oz sugar to each 1 lb of sloes. Cover with gin, seal firmly and shake well to dissolve the sugar. Keep in a warm place and shake each day for several weeks. After 3 months, strain the liqueur through coffee filter papers or muslin into clean sterilised bottles, seal well and leave to mature. More sugar can be added later if the liqueur is too sour for personal taste. This drink improves with keeping.

Blackberry or Gooseberry Ale

This is easy to make and produces a strong beer with a rich fruity flavour.

1 lb ripe blackberries   **1 lb sugar**
or gooseberries   **3 pints strong ale (not barley wine)**
1 sachet ale yeast

Wash and dry the berries and if using gooseberries chop them roughly. Place the berries in a large, wide-necked sterilised jar. Dissolve the sugar in the ale and pour over the berries. Stir in the yeast and cover loosely. Leave in a warm place to ferment. When fermentation has finished, move the beer to a cool place to settle, then siphon into bottles and seal with pop-off plastic caps. Store in a cool dark place for 3 months before drinking. If a wide-necked jar is not available the yeast could be stirred into the sugar/ale mixture before pouring over the berries.

     'The Meadow Path' by Theresa S. Stannard

Simple Strawberry Wine

Strawberries lose much of their elusive flavour when made into wine. This method retains the scented fragrance of the fruit.

2 lb strawberries   8 oz caster sugar
White wine or sherry to cover

Place alternate layers of strawberries and sugar in a sterile jar, filling it right to the top. Pour the wine or sherry slowly over the fruit to cover, ensuring there are no air bubbles between the layers. Seal tightly and store in a cool dry place for 4-6 weeks. When ready, strain the liquid into a sterilised bottle and seal tightly. The type of sherry used is according to preference or availability, but medium sherry is generally suitable.

Potato Wine

Potato wine, like parsnip wine, is one of the most traditional home-produced country wines and can possess quite a kick.

2 lb potatoes, scrubbed well	1 pint fresh wheat, husks removed
2 lb raisins, washed in	6 pints water
hot water and chopped	Wine yeast
4 lb brown sugar	Campden tablet

Sprinkle the yeast granules into a cup of boiled tepid water, cover with clingfilm and leave to stand for about an hour. Grate the potatoes into a fermentation bin then stir in the raisins, sugar and wheat. Bring the water to the boil, pour over the ingredients and stir well until all the sugar has dissolved. Cover and leave to cool. When cool, add the activated yeast, cover loosely and keep in a cool place for 3 weeks, stirring at regular intervals. Strain the liquid into a demi-john topping up to 1 gallon with cold boiled water if required. Fit an airlock and leave to ferment. When fermentation has ceased, siphon the wine into a clean demi-john and add 1 crushed Campden tablet. Bung tight and store for at least six months. Finally, siphon into sterilised bottles, seal tightly and then, before drinking, take care to judge the potency of the brew!

Ginger Beer

Ginger beer, which is sweet with a strong ginger flavour, first became popular in the nineteenth century. This recipe is mildly alcoholic.

'GINGER BEER PLANT'
½ oz dried yeast   **½ pint water**   **Sugar**
Ground ginger   **Juice of 2 lemons**

Put the yeast into a jar, add the water, 2 teaspoons sugar and 2 teaspoons ground ginger and mix well. Cover the jar with a lid or clingfilm. Each day for 7 days add 1 teaspoon sugar and 1 teaspoon ground ginger. Finally, strain the mixture, add the lemon juice to the liquid and reserve the sediment. The liquid is now ready to use. For future use (or to give to a friend), keep the sediment and divide it equally between 2 jars. To each jar add ½ pint water, 2 teaspoons sugar and 2 teaspoons ginger and proceed all over again, as previously, ad infinitum.

2 oz sugar   **Cold boiled water**   **'Ginger beer plant' liquid**

Add the sugar to the 'ginger beer plant' liquid and make up to 1 gallon with water, stirring until the sugar has dissolved completely. Pour into strong, dark coloured beer bottles and cap with pop-off plastic caps; (these will pop off safely if the bottles become dangerously pressurised). Leave for 7 to 10 days before drinking.

Rosehip Wine

Rosehips of all varieties should be collected whole. then cleaned and chopped. Do not liquidise or mince them too finely, as this will spoil the flavour of the wine.

2 lb fresh rosehips (or ½ lb dried)	**1 teaspoon citric acid**
8 oz raisins, hot washed and finely chopped	**4 teaspoons grape tannin or**
3 lb sugar	**a cup of strong tea**
6 pints boiling water	**1 teaspoon pectin enzyme**
Wine yeast	**Campden tablets**
1 teaspoon yeast nutrient	**1 teaspoon potassium sorbate**

Sprinkle yeast granules into a cup of boiled tepid water, cover and leave to stand for about an hour. Rinse rosehips in a solution of 2 Campden tablets to 1¾ pints water. Drain and chop them coarsely. Place the rosehips, raisins, sugar, yeast nutrient, citric acid and tannin or tea in a fermentation bin and pour over the boiling water. Stir well to dissolve the sugar, cover and leave to cool until lukewarm. Add activated yeast and pectin enzyme and cover again. Stir daily for 8 days, then strain into a demi-john and fit bung and airlock. Leave to stand until wine clears, then siphon wine off sediment into a clean demi-john adding 1 crushed Campden tablet and the potassium sorbate and top up with cold boiled water if necessary, to shoulder of demi-john. Bung tightly and leave for 3 months. Siphon into sterilised bottles, seal tightly and store in cool, dark place.

Gooseberry Ratafia

A clear, sweet, slightly spicy drink which is superb with cheese.

2 lb ripe gooseberries   **4 cloves, bruised**
1 cinnamon stick   **1 standard bottle gin or vodka**
10 oz caster sugar

Wash and mash the gooseberries to a purée (this can be done in a food processor). Put the pulp into a fine mesh nylon bag and squeeze out all the juice. Discard the pulp. Mix the juice with the spices, gin or vodka and about 4 oz sugar in a sterilised jar. Seal tightly and leave in a cool, dark place for 4 weeks. When ready, siphon the clear liquid off the sediment into a bowl, stir in the rest of the sugar until dissolved and then pour into sterilised bottles. Keep for 1 month before drinking.

Dandelion Wine

The sunny, yellow and ubiquitous dandelion flowers bloom profusely from April onwards; St. George's Day, 23rd April is traditionally the day to pick them.

2 pts dandelion flowers	1 teaspoon yeast nutrient
3 pints boiling water	1 heaped teaspoon tartaric acid
3 lb sugar	1 pint cold boiled water
1 lb sultanas, rinsed in hot	Wine yeast
water and finely chopped	Campden tablet

Sprinkle yeast into ⅔ of mug of warm water and stir in 1 teaspoon sugar. Cover and leave in warm place until needed. Put the flowers into a fermentation bin and pour over the 3 pints of boiling water. Add sugar, stirring until completely dissolved. Add sultanas, yeast nutrient and tartaric acid and stir again. Add cold water, cover and leave until cool. When cool (70°-75°F) stir in activated yeast. Cover and leave in warm place for 4 to 5 days, stirring daily. When ready, strain the liquid into a demi-john, fit an airlock and leave to ferment. When fermentation is finished and liquid is starting to clear from surface, siphon wine off sediment into a demi-john. Add a crushed Campden tablet, top up jar with more cold boiled water if necessary to the 1 gallon mark and leave to clear for few weeks. When wine is bright and clear, siphon into sterilised bottles, seal tightly and store in cool place.

'Ducks a dabbling' by H. Sylvester Stannard

Lavender 'Champagne'

A delicious and unusual fizzy drink for a summer day. Make sure that the flowers are free from traffic fumes, insecticides and pesticides. Shake the flowers gently to dislodge any insects.

40 lavender flowers	**4 oz sultanas, finely chopped**
3¾ pints cold boiled water	**2 tablespoons white wine vinegar**
11 oz sugar	**Juice of 1 lemon**

In a large glass or china container, stir all the dry ingredients together. Pour on the water, wine vinegar and lemon juice and stir well. Cover the container with a lid and leave for 7 days. When ready, strain the liquid into sterilised bottles and seal with pop-off plastic caps. Leave for another week, by which time the liquid should be sparkling.

Blackberry Syrup

A pleasant nightcap that is also said to be good for relieving a cold.

1 lb blackberries	**½ lb sugar**
½ pint white wine vinegar	**4 oz honey**

Place the blackberries in a glass or china bowl and pour the vinegar over. Leave to stand for at least 24 hours, stirring and pressing the fruit regularly, to extract the juices. Strain the liquid into a large saucepan or small preserving pan and bring to the boil. Add the sugar, stirring until it is all dissolved, then add the honey, stirring well. Bring back to the boil and boil hard for 5 minutes. Allow to cool completely. Originally this syrup was bottled and stored; one tablespoon being added to a glass of hot water to form a bedtime drink. However, the syrup can easily be frozen in ice-cube trays and then stored in bags in the freezer to be used when required.

Lemonade

This homemade lemonade bears no resemblance to the fizzy variety of lemonade sold in the shops today. It is a delicious, refreshing drink well worth the minimal effort involved to make it.

3 lemons	**2 tablespoons honey**
3 oz caster sugar	**1½ pints boiling water**

Wash the lemons and remove the zest only, with a potato peeler or small, sharp knife. Squeeze the lemons and strain the juice to remove the pips. Put the lemon zest, sugar and honey into a large heatproof bowl. Pour the boiling water over and stir to dissolve the sugar. Cover and leave until cold. Strain the liquid into a large jug and add the lemon juice. Serve chilled.

Cider Toddy

*This makes a warming drink to enjoy on a cold winter evening and is
also very reviving at the end of a long day.*

½ pint dry cider   **A strip of lemon rind**
A piece of fresh root ginger   **1 tablespoon clear honey**

Put the cider, ginger and lemon rind into a pan and heat until hot, but not boiling.
Stir in the honey, strain into a warmed, strong glass or mug and drink hot.

Cherry Brandy

*As Charles Dickens wrote, Kent is famous for cherries and the county
has also long been known for its cherry brandy.It is one of the
great English liqueurs and is easy to make.*

Morello cherries	**Caster sugar**
Brandy	**Cloves (optional)**

The cherries should be gathered in dry weather. Wipe them with a dry cloth and remove the stalks. Prick each cherry with a darning needle and three-quarters fill wide-necked bottles. Add sugar to the fruit, allowing 3 oz of sugar to every 1 lb of fruit. Top up each bottle with brandy; if desired, 3 or 4 cloves may be added to each bottle before securing the top. Shake occasionally and keep for 2 months before use.

Parsley Wine

A delightful herb wine which is particularly good as an accompaniment to fish dishes.

1 lb parsley leaves (no stalks)	Cold boiled water for topping up
2 lemons	Wine yeast and nutrient
1 lb sultanas hot washed and chopped	2½ lb sugar
1 gallon water	Campden tablet

Sprinkle yeast granules and nutrient into cup of boiled tepid water, cover and leave for about an hour. Strip parsley leaves from stalks; take care not to include any stalks. Wash well, chop and put into large pan. Thinly peel lemons, avoiding white pith and place rind in pan with parsley. Add gallon of water and heat until boiling, then simmer for 10 minutes. Place sultanas in fermentation bin and strain over parsley liquid. Discard parsley and lemon rind. Top up to 1 gallon with cold, boiled water and leave to cool. When cool add lemon juice and activated yeast/nutrient. Cover loosely and leave for 5 days to ferment. Strain mixture, pressing sultanas to extract as much liquid as possible, then discard. Add sugar to liquid, stirring until dissolved then pour into demi-john and fit airlock. Leave to ferment at temperature about 18°C/64°F. When fermentation finished, siphon clearing wine into clean demi-john, adding 1 crushed Campden tablet. Bung tight and store for 3 months in cool place. Siphon into sterilised bottles, seal tightly and store.

'A Cottage Home" by Theresa S. Stannard

Strawberry Ratafia

In the eighteenth century a ratafia was a liqueur flavoured with peach or apricot kernels, but by the Victorian era it had come to mean a fruit steeped in a sweetened spirit. This liqueur is a lovely pink colour with a wonderful flavour.

5 lb strawberries   1 lb caster sugar
1 standard bottle vodka

Put the fruit in a large bowl and sprinkle over the sugar. Mash the mixture to a pulp. Cover and leave to stand overnight. Next day, pack the mashed strawberries into a sterilised jar. Cover with vodka and seal tightly. Store in a cool, dark place for 5 days, shaking the jar daily. When ready, strain the liquid through coffee filter papers or muslin into bottles and seal tightly. Leave for a few weeks before drinking.

Walnut Wine

Gather the walnuts at the end of June or early July, when they are formed but still green and the shells inside are still soft.

8 green walnuts	**7 oz caster sugar**
1 cinnamon stick, halved	**1¾ pints robust red wine**
1 vanilla pod, halved	**4 fl oz dark rum or brandy**

Wash and dry the walnuts and cut them into small pieces. Place them in a large, sterilised glass jar with the cinnamon and vanilla. Cover with the sugar, wine and rum or brandy. Seal the jar tightly and leave for 6 weeks, shaking the jar lightly from time to time to ensure the sugar has dissolved completely. When ready, strain the liquid through a coffee filter paper or muslin into sterilised bottles and seal tightly. Keep in a cool, dark place.

Beetroot Beer

*A simple old country recipe, which produces a somewhat sweet drink with
a dark rich, full-bodied taste without any hint of beetroot. The beetroot
is not peeled as much of the goodness lies in the skin.*

**1 lb beetroot   1 pint stout
8oz unrefined dark muscovado sugar**

Scrub the beetroots, cut into slices and put into a bowl. Sprinkle over the sugar,
cover and set aside for 24 hours. When ready strain the off the liquid and add it to
the stout. Put into bottles and seal with pop-off plastic caps. Leave for 7-14 days
before drinking.

Redcurrant Shrub

Shrub was popular in the eighteenth and nineteenth centuries and was made from a spirit combined with fruit juice and sugar. The word comes from the Arabic word 'shurb' meaning drink.

½ pint redcurrant juice   1 pint white rum or brandy
7 oz sugar

Put the redcurrant juice and rum or brandy into a sterilised jar. Add the sugar and seal tightly. Leave in a cool, dark place for at least 4 weeks, shaking frequently. Strain into sterilised bottles, seal tightly and store in a cool, dark place. The redcurrant juice can either be purchased ready for use or made by liquidising approx. 1 lb of redcurrants with just a little water in a processor or blender then straining to remove the skins and seeds.

Ginger Wine

This wine is quite strong. It is a tonic which is soothing to sore throats and colds.

3 oz root ginger
3 lemons
1 lb raisins, hot washed and chopped
Pinch of cayenne pepper

7 pints boiling water
All purpose wine yeast and nutrient
3 lb unrefined Demerara sugar
Campden tablet

Bruise the ginger. Thinly peel the lemons, being careful to avoid including the white pith. Squeeze the juice from the lemons and strain to remove the pips. Sprinkle the yeast granules and nutrient into a cup of boiled tepid water, cover with clingfilm and leave to stand for about an hour. Put the ginger, lemon rind and raisins into a fermentation bin with the cayenne and pour on the boiling water. Stir well, then cover and leave until cool. Add the activated yeast to the bin with the lemon juice and stir. Cover the bin loosely and ferment for 7 days. Strain the mixture, pressing out the solids, then discard these. Stir in 1 lb sugar and pour into a demi-john. Fit an airlock and leave to ferment for 1 week. Decant half the wine from the jar and stir in another 1 lb sugar, then return the wine to the demi-john. After another week, repeat the process with the rest of the sugar and leave to ferment. When fermentation has ceased, siphon the cleared wine into a demi-john and add 1 crushed Campden tablet. Siphon off into sterilised bottles and store for 6 months before drinking.

Lavender Liqueur

The delightful fragrance of lavender is here used to make a delicious drink which is excellent taken after dinner as a digestive or trickled over ice-cream. Avoid flowers that have been treated with insecticides and pesticides or polluted with traffic fumes. Shake the flowers gently to dislodge any insects.

50 lavender flowers	**1 teaspoon aniseed**
4 oz rose petals	**Pinch ground cinnamon**
1 teaspoon coriander seeds	**1 standard bottle brandy**

Remove the white bases from the rose petals (these are bitter) and pack all the ingredients into a sterilised jar. Cover with brandy and seal tightly. Store in a cool, dark place for 6 months, shaking the jar occasionally. When ready, strain the liquid into sterilised bottles and seal tightly. Store in a cool, dark place.

Kentish Winter Cordial

Country housewives used to make fruit or flower syrups to ward off colds and chills. Diluted with water and drunk hot, they sooth sore throats and aid sleep.

1¾ pints damsons   1 pint elderberries
1¾ pints water   4 cloves
4 lb unrefined light muscovado sugar

Remove the stones from the damsons and crack 12 of them. Put into a large pan and pour the water over the damsons and cracked stones. Cover and leave for 24 hours. Next day, heat the fruit and water until boiling, then boil for 15 minutes. Remove from the heat and strain the liquid over the elderberries in a large bowl. Cover and leave to stand for 24 hours. Pour back into a pan, add the cloves and bring to boiling point. Add the sugar and simmer for 10 minutes, stirring, until the sugar has dissolved. Remove from the heat, set aside and leave until completely cold. Remove the cloves, pour the wine into sterilised bottles and seal tightly. Dilute with hot water to serve.

Honey Beer

Long before the Romans arrived in Britain, Druid bards described the island as "The Isle of Honey". After the Roman invasion, Pliny noted that 'these islanders consume copious quantities of the honeybrew'. Honey continued to be used to make beer for hundreds of years, until it was superseded by grain and hop based ales.

1 lemon	1 gallon water
1½ lb dark honey	½ oz hops
1 teaspoon granulated yeast	

Peel the rind from the lemon, avoiding the white pith. Squeeze the juice from the lemon and strain to remove the pips. Dissolve the honey in 1¾ pints of the water in a bucket. Put the rest of the water into a large pan with the hops and lemon rind, bring to the boil and boil for 30 minutes. Strain the hop water into the honey solution and leave to cool. Discard the hops and lemon rind. Add the yeast and lemon juice to the cooled mixture, cover over and leave for 3-4 days in a warm place to ferment. When fermentation has ceased, siphon into sterilised 1 pint beer bottles, leaving an airspace at the top. Add ½ level teaspoon sugar to each bottle. Seal with plastic pop-off caps and leave in a warm room to ferment for a few days. Then store for at least 2 weeks in a cool, dark place before drinking.

Barley Water

*Barley water is both refreshing served on a hot day and nourishing
and traditionally was served to invalids.*

1 tablespoon pearl barley   **8 teaspoons sugar**
Peel of 4 lemons, avoiding white pith **4 pints boiling water**

Put the pearl barley into a large bowl and scald it by pouring over boiling water.
Then strain the barley and discard the water. Put the scalded barley into a large bowl
with the peel of the 4 lemons cut into strips, and the 8 teaspoons of sugar. Pour 4
pints of boiling water over the barley mixture, cover and leave to cool. When cold,
pour slowly into a jug to leave behind the sediment but do not strain it off. The
squeezed juice of a lemon may be added to the jug before serving.

'Beside the Arun at Fittleworth Bridge' by H. Sylvester Stannard

Herb Liqueur

A delicious digestive drink which combines herbs, flowers and spices. The herbs and flowers can be changed according to whatever is available and edible. Ensure they are not poisonous!

1 pint gin or vodka	5 juniper berries
12 oz caster sugar	4 cloves
15 fl oz boiling water	Pinch tea leaves
1 small orange	4 bay leaves
Thinly peeled rind 1 lemon	2 sprigs rosemary
2 cinnamon sticks	3 sage leaves
1 vanilla pod	2 sprigs thyme
4 cardamom pods	1 tablespoon dried elderflowers

1 tablespoon dried lemon verbena

First, put all the ingredients except the sugar, water and gin or vodka into a large sterilised jar then pour on the spirit, making sure the dry ingredients are submerged under the spirit. Cover and leave to infuse for 1 month. Dissolve the sugar in the boiling water and leave to cool. Strain the herb mixture into the cool sugar syrup and stir well. Pour into a sterilised jar and leave for another month. Finally, strain through coffee filter papers or muslin into sterilised bottles and seal tightly.

Blackberry Wine

One of the great traditional country wines. Use only large black fruits that are fully ripe. This makes a strong, sweet wine.

3 lb blackberries	**4 lb sugar**
8 oz raisins, washed in	**1 teaspoon pectin enzyme**
hot water and chopped	**Bordeaux wine yeast and nutrient**
1 gallon boiling water	**Campden tablet**

Wash the berries in a Campden solution, then drain and crush them. Place the berries in a fermentation bin with the raisins and sugar. Pour over the boiling water and leave to cool to lukewarm. Add the yeast, nutrient and pectin enzyme, then cover and leave in a warm place for 5 days, stirring twice daily. Strain into a demijohn and fit a bung and an airlock. When fermentation has ceased, siphon into a clean demi-john, add the crushed Campden tablet and leave to stand. As soon as the wine is clear, siphon into sterilised bottles, seal tightly and store in a cool, dark place for 6 months before drinking.

Cowslip Wine

In days gone by a glass of cowslip wine was drunk at bedtime to encourage a restful night's sleep. Dried cowslip flowers are available from herbalists.

2 lemons	**1 gallon boiling water**
2 oz dried cowslip flowers	**1 lb sugar**
1 lb sultanas, washed in hot	**Wine yeast and nutrient**
water and chopped	**Campden tablet**

Sprinkle the yeast granules and nutrient into a cup of boiled tepid water, cover with clingfilm and leave to stand for about an hour. Thinly peel the lemons, avoiding the white pith. Chop the rind into small pieces and squeeze and strain the juice. Put the flowers and lemon rind into a fermentation bin and pour on one gallon of boiling water. Add the sultanas and sugar, stirring until the sugar is dissolved. Cover and leave to cool. When cool add the activated yeast and nutrient with the lemon juice and cover loosely. Leave to ferment for 4 days, keeping the flowers submerged with a large non-metal plate or similar. Strain the mixture, pressing the flowers to extract all the liquid and pour into a demi-john. Fit an airlock and leave to ferment. When fermentation has finished, siphon the wine into a clean demi-john and add 1 crushed Campden tablet. Bung tight and store for 3 months. Siphon into sterilised bottles, seal tightly and store in a cool place.

'Gathering Cowslips at Upper Slaughter' by H. Sylvester Stannard

Treacle Ale

*This is a traditional recipe from Scotland. The treacle gives the beer
a strong, slightly bitter flavour.*

1 lemon	**1 lb golden syrup**
8 oz black treacle	**1 gallon boiled warm water**
1 teaspoon granulated yeast	

Peel the lemon thinly, avoiding all the white pith. Squeeze the juice from the lemon
and strain to remove the pips. Dissolve the treacle and golden syrup in the warm
water in a bucket and then add the lemon rind. Cover and leave to cool. Stir in the
lemon juice and the yeast, then cover loosely and leave for 36 hours in a warm room.
When ready, skim off the froth and siphon the beer into sterilised strong beer
bottles, creating as little froth as possible. Seal with plastic pop-off caps; these will
pop off if the bottles become dangerously pressurised. Store for 7 days in a cool
place before drinking.

Raspberry Liqueur

Sweet, spirit-based drinks flavoured with fruits, herbs and spices originated in the late Middle Ages. Recipes were frequently devised by monks for medicinal purposes and their ingredients were closely guarded secrets.

10 oz ripe raspberries   **1 pint hot (boiled) water**
1 standard bottle gin or vodka   **10 oz white sugar**

Place the raspberries in a sterilised jar and pour on the gin or vodka. Seal tightly and leave in a warm place for 1 week, shaking the jar every day. Dissolve the sugar in the hot, boiled water until completely dissolved and leave to cool. Strain the raspberry gin or vodka through a fine strainer or coffee filter paper on to the cool syrup and stir well. Pour through a funnel into 2 sterilised bottles. Seal tightly and store for a few weeks before drinking.

Elderflower Wine

Scented elderflowers can be used fresh or dried for this recipe. Use only fresh flowers with a sweet perfume and shake gently before using, to dislodge any insects.

6 large heads elderflowers in full bloom	**1½ lb sugar**
	1 pint boiling water
8 oz sultanas, washed in hot water and chopped	**5 pints cold boiled water**
	Yeast and nutrient
Zest and juice of 2 lemons	**Campden tablet**

Remove the flowers from the stems; do not include any green stems as they will make the wine bitter. Wash gently in a sterilising solution and dry them. Dissolve the sugar in the boiling water and leave to cool. Sprinkle the yeast and nutrient over half a cup of tepid water, cover and leave in a warm place. Place the flowers in a fermentation bin with the lemon juice and zest. Add the sultanas and sugar and the cold water. Stir well, then add the activated yeast. Cover and leave in a warm place, stirring twice each day for 3-4 days. Strain into a demi-john and make up to a gallon if necessary, with cold boiled water. Fit a bung and an airlock and leave to ferment. When fermentation is finished, move to a cool place for a few days to help it clear. Siphon off the clearing wine into a demi-john and add 1 crushed Campden tablet. Bung tight and store in a cool place until bright and clear, then siphon into sterilised bottles, seal tightly and keep for 3 months before using.

'The Boathouse' by Theresa S. Stannard

General Information

Making wines and beers at home has greatly changed over recent years. Today, inexpensive beginner's kits are available from home brew suppliers and contain all the equipment and instructions needed to start off the novice.

The equipment needed for wine and beer making is quite simple. **A fermentation bin** made of food grade plastic with a lid. This is to ferment the pulped fruit or flowers, which must be kept submerged and loosely covered to keep out dust and flies and also allow the fermentation gas to escape. When the wine or beer has ceased bubbling and there is no more activity, then fermentation has finished and the liquid can be siphoned off the sediment. **Two demi-johns** (glass jars with two 'ears') to ferment the wine. **A fermentation lock**. When in use it is essential to half-fill the airlock with water to create a seal. **A demi-john bung** with a hole for the fermentation lock to fit into. Also solid bungs to seal the demi-johns. **Siphon tubing** to siphon off the wine from the sediment. This is done by placing the demi-john containing the fermented wine higher than the demi-john into which the wine is to be siphoned, e.g. placed on a table. **A plastic funnel: A nylon bottle brush: A plastic spoon with a long handle: New corks and pop-off plastic caps: Bottles: Campden tablets**. A good supply of these will be needed as they are used to sterilise the equipment before use (essential) and for clearing the wine before bottling and to prevent bacterial infection: **Pectin destroying enzyme**. Some fruit wines contain a lot of pectin (the substance which causes jam to set). This is not wanted in winemaking and it must be destroyed. **Bentonite**. Sometimes needed (depending on the type of wine) to remove the haze that remains in the wine. **Yeast**. Special yeasts are now available, cultured from pure yeast cells taken from grapes grown in wine producing regions. These are often a specific type, e.g. Champagne or Bordeaux and are much superior to and more reliable than bakers' and brewers' yeasts. Granulated wine yeasts are sold in sealed sachets and usually have nutrient salts added to provide just the right amount of nourishment for the yeast, to ensure good fermentation. One sachet is all that is needed for each wine recipe. Both yeast and nutrient can be bought separately.

Beer making equipment is much the same except, instead of a demi-john, only a fermentation bin or bucket will be needed. Also always use beer bottles; never use wine or lemonade bottles or similar thin glass containers. Beer can generate enormous pressure and can cause these types of bottles to explode! One sachet of yeast is sufficient for each beer recipe. When siphoning beer into bottles, it is essential to leave an airspace at the top of each one to allow for the pressure from secondary fermentation which occurs in the bottles after priming. Priming sugar is added, not more than ½ teaspoon per 1 pint of beer. Less than this makes the beer lifeless; too much and the beer will be too gassy. An alternative, more modern, method is to add the priming sugar, dissolved in a little hot water, to the beer after fermentation in the bucket and immediately before siphoning into bottles. After priming, seal the bottles with pop-off plastic caps and leave in a warm room for a few days to ferment, then store in a cool place for a few weeks to mature.

It is essential to clean thoroughly and to sterilise all equipment (including corks and bottle caps) before starting. There are several excellent sterilisers to choose from, e.g. Chempro, which come with full instructions. It is also essential to wash fruit and vegetables in a Campden solution to sterilise them. Dissolve 4 tablets in 4 pints water. Be sure always to label and date all bottles as soon as they are sealed. Always make sure that all blooms used are free from traffic fumes, insecticides and pesticides. If in doubt, buy the flowers from a herbalist.

The weights and measures used in the preceding recipes can be easily converted to their metric equivalents. The conversions listed below are only approximate, having been rounded up or down as may be appropriate.

Weights

Avoirdupois	Metric
1 oz.	just under 30 grams
4 oz. (¼ lb.)	app. 115 grams
8 oz. (½ lb.)	app. 230 grams
1 lb.	454 grams

Liquid Measures

Imperial	Metric
1 fl. oz.	app. 30 millilitres
¼ pt	app. 145 millilitres
½ pt.	app. 285 millilitres
1 pt.	app. 570 millilitres
1¾ pt.	app. 1 litre
1 gall.	app. 4.5 litres